Train Your Brain with Collaboration Activities

THINK LIKE A PROGRAMMER

by Emilee Hillman

illustrated by Dana Regan

Published in 2020 by Cavendish Square Publishing, LLC
243 5th Avenue, Suite 136, New York, NY 10016

Website: cavendishsq.com

This publication represents the opinions and views of the author based on his or her personal
experience, knowledge, and research. The information in this book serves as a general
guide only. The author and publisher have used their best efforts in preparing this book and
disclaim liability rising directly or indirectly from the use and application of this book.

All websites were available and accurate when this book was sent to press.

Library of Congress Cataloging-in-Publication Data

Names: Hillman, Emilee, author. | Regan, Dana.
Title: Train your brain with collaboration activities / Emilee Hillman; illustrator Dana Regan.
Description: First edition. | New York : Cavendish Square, 2020. | Series: Think like a
programmer. | Includes bibliographical references and index. | Audience: Grade 2 to 5.
Identifiers: LCCN 2018059097 (print) | LCCN 2019006481 (ebook) | ISBN 9781502648136 (ebook) |
ISBN 9781502648129 (library bound) | ISBN 9781502648105 (pbk.) | ISBN 9781502648112 (6 pack)
Subjects: LCSH: Computer programming--Juvenile literature. | Problem solving--
Juvenile literature. | Cooperativeness--Juvenile literature.
Classification: LCC QA76.52 (ebook) | LCC QA76.52 .H545 2020 (print) | DDC 005.1--dc23
LC record available at https://lccn.loc.gov/2018059097

Editorial Director: David McNamara
Editor: Kristen Susienka
Copy Editor: Nathan Heidelberger
Associate Art Director: Alan Sliwinski
Designer: Joe Parenteau
Illustrator: Dana Regan
Production Coordinator: Karol Szymczuk

Printed in the United States of America

Contents

INTRODUCTION 4

DOWN AND ACROSS 6

A GROUP TALE 8

COLLABORATION DRAWING 10

MEASURED GUESSING 12

CENTI-INCHES 14

PAPER CHAIN 16

PENNY BRIDGE 18

COLUMN WRITING 20

APPRECIATION 22

CITATION NEEDED 24

SOCIAL MEDIA SAFETY 26

PRIVACY AND SHARING 28

GLOSSARY 30

FIND OUT MORE 31

INDEX 32

Introduction

You want to be a computer programmer—great! The best programmers understand how to put ideas together, test their ideas, and work together when needed. The activities in this book will help you understand how to work together to think through problems.

This is all part of **computational thinking**. Despite the name, this way of thinking doesn't need a computer! All you have to do is think about how to solve problems, one step at a time.

These fun activities will help you train your brain to work through problems step by step. Some activities will have you work with a partner. Others will help you learn about how to work with many other people. Some activities will also talk about **digital citizenship**. Through it all, you'll learn the best ways to think like a programmer!

Down and Across

NUMBER OF PLAYERS **2 OR MORE**

TIME NEEDED

20–30 minutes

ACTIVITY OVERVIEW

When programmers face a difficult piece of code, they often ask their friends to help them. Computational thinking works best when many people work on the same problem to

You'll Need
- Pencil
- Paper

find a great solution. In this activity, you and some partners will work together on a project.

INSTRUCTIONS

First, an **acrostic** is a word that is split into other words, such as:

My friends are

C aring

O pen

O utgoing

L ots of fun

In this activity, everyone has to write their own acrostic! After everyone comes up with a different word they want to spell, everyone should write their word on a piece of paper. Each player should then come up with words that start with each letter. The words should connect to the main word you choose. Follow the example above if you get stuck. When you are done, read your acrostics to each other.

A Group Tale

NUMBER OF PLAYERS **2 OR MORE**

TIME NEEDED

20–30 minutes

You'll Need
- Pencil
- Paper

ACTIVITY OVERVIEW

One thing that all good computational thinkers know is that they don't know everything. Sometimes they need to work together to solve a problem. Even the best programmers in the world work on teams. Teamwork often leads to the best solution. Great solutions are often reached when many people work together. In this activity, you and some partners will work together to write a story.

INSTRUCTIONS

First, one player should begin by writing a story starter at the top of a blank piece of paper. An example of how to start could be, "Once upon a

time in a dark forest ..."
Then, the next player
should write one
sentence continuing
the story. Taking turns,
each player should add
one sentence to the
story until it is finished.
Each person should
write their sentence
without asking the
group what to do! That
way, the story is more
unique. When the story
is complete, read the
whole thing together!

THINK ABOUT IT!

Working together on one project is an important skill in computational thinking. If you want to take this activity farther, you and your partners can do it again. This time, though, split up the work. One person can come up with the characters. The next person can invent where the story takes place. Another person can come up with a time period the story happens in. Then work together to write the story using these rules and the steps in the first activity.

Collaboration Drawing

NUMBER OF PLAYERS 1

TIME NEEDED

15–20 minutes

ACTIVITY OVERVIEW

Working in teams and developing group skills are important in both **computer science** and computational thinking. Coding can be very difficult. However, some of the best answers happen when strong thinkers work together. In this activity, you will think about and illustrate teamwork.

INSTRUCTIONS

First, write a short paragraph. This paragraph should talk about a time when students in your class (or a group of your friends) worked together to solve a problem or work through a task. Write about what

the problem or task was. Who worked with you to solve or complete it? What was the end result? Once your paragraph is done, draw pictures of your story. The pictures should show how everyone working together made the task or problem easier.

Measured Guessing

NUMBER OF PLAYERS

TIME NEEDED

20–30 minutes

ACTIVITY OVERVIEW

Computational thinkers usually work toward figuring something out exactly. However, some of the best code begins with nothing but a guess! Great programmers might not have the answers right away, but they can start with ideas and guesses and work forward from there. In this activity, you will have to make guesses.

INSTRUCTIONS

To begin, choose some small objects around your house. Ideas are a pen, a toy, or a cell phone. Then, try to guess how long each object is. After you write down your guesses, find a ruler and double-check your work. Write the real answers down. Were you close to the right answers?

THINK ABOUT IT!

You can repeat this activity for many different kinds of household objects. You can also try guessing and then measuring larger objects. Try guessing how long your kitchen table is. Then, measure one part of the table. Do you want to change your guess now that you know how long one part is? Now measure the whole table. Were you right?

Centi-Inches

NUMBER OF PLAYERS 2

TIME NEEDED

20–30 minutes

ACTIVITY OVERVIEW

Computational thinkers like working together because they know there are so many ways of looking at a problem. One person's solution may not be the best! Often, the most correct answer comes when many people work together. In this activity, you and a friend will test each other.

INSTRUCTIONS

First, find a ruler to use to measure. Then, go around your house and measure objects. Ideas are a pen, a tablet, or a cell phone. Measure each object one at a time. There's a catch, however: one of you must measure in inches, and the other in centimeters! Each of you should write your answers down on a separate piece of paper. Make sure your friend can't see your answers. Then, compare your answers. One of you will have to change your measurements to inches or centimeters to see if the measurements match!

Paper Chain

NUMBER OF PLAYERS

TIME NEEDED

20–30 minutes

You'll Need
- Pencil
- Paper
- Scissors
- Tape
- Ruler

ACTIVITY OVERVIEW

Many times, computational thinking has lots of trial and error. There are usually many ways to approach a problem. There is rarely one solution. Not all of the ways will be the best or easiest. Not all of them will give the right answer either. Strong computational thinkers keep trying new ways until they find a good way to solve the problem. In this activity, you will make a chain from paper.

INSTRUCTIONS

You will make a paper chain that is at least 24 inches (60 centimeters) long. First, write down or draw your design. How do you want it to look? Then, use paper, scissors, and tape to make the paper chain. You need to guess at how many links will make 24 inches. After you have your chain put together, test it out! Use a ruler to check your progress. Is the chain too long? Too short? Make some changes. Try again. You should do this as many times as it takes to get to 24 inches. Afterward, think about how you would build a chain 36 inches (90 cm) long.

Penny Bridge

NUMBER OF PLAYERS 1

TIME NEEDED

20–30 minutes

ACTIVITY OVERVIEW

Computational thinkers often have to try a few ideas before they find one that solves their problem. Sometimes, they find a new way of solving a problem while they are testing a different idea. In this activity, you will build a bridge.

INSTRUCTIONS

First, ask your parents or an adult for a roll of pennies. Then, look at the pennies. How could you build a bridge of pennies between two piles of pennies? Draw some different designs for the bridge. Once you have your designs drawn, try to

build the bridge! As you build, don't be afraid to
try new designs or make changes to your ideas.
This might happen if your idea isn't working or if you
have a different idea while building.

Column Writing

NUMBER OF PLAYERS 1

TIME NEEDED

20–30 minutes

ACTIVITY OVERVIEW

One of the many strengths of computational thinkers is their ability to think of great solutions, even if things limit what they can do. For example, **coders** might have to follow certain rules to make their programs. There are often many obstacles between the start of a project and the end of a project. However, computational thinking can help overcome them. In this activity, you will work around a serious demand.

INSTRUCTIONS

Begin by thinking of what makes a good friend. Then, write your thoughts down—but with a catch! The first words on the left-hand side of the paper should spell "FRIEND," going down. Try to come up with words that start with each letter and describe a good friend. This is called an acrostic. Can you then do the activity again but come up with different words to describe "FRIEND"?

Appreciation

NUMBER OF PLAYERS ● 1

TIME NEEDED

15–20 minutes

You'll Need
- Pencil
- Drawing supplies
- Paper

ACTIVITY OVERVIEW

Working together is an important skill all coders should learn. Often the best coders in the world can't finish their amazing software designs without help from others. They know it is important to thank these supporters for everything they do! In this activity, you will thank someone who has helped you.

INSTRUCTIONS

First, think of someone who helps you or your friends out. A few ideas are a teacher, a coach—or your parents! After coming up with your helper, draw a picture of that person helping you. Then, write

a few sentences beneath your drawing. These sentences should describe how the person helps you, why they help you, and why you appreciate them! And remember to say thank you.

It is not always easy to really appreciate someone. To build on this activity, think about what actions the person in your drawing does for you or helps you do. Then, do those actions for the person! For example, if you say your parents are helpful because they cook dinner, you could cook them dinner. By doing this, you'll be able to appreciate the person better.

Citation Needed

NUMBER OF PLAYERS 4 OR MORE

TIME NEEDED

20–30 minutes

ACTIVITY OVERVIEW

You'll Need
- Pencil
- Drawing supplies
- Paper

In the digital world, a lot of information is available to anyone who looks. Every piece of **data** online was created by someone. Those people deserve to be thanked whenever their work is used. Computational thinkers know that reusing other people's work is extremely helpful. They also know that they need to list those people by name. In this activity, you and some partners will learn about **citations**.

INSTRUCTIONS

First, get some friends together! Then, each of you should draw a picture on a blank piece of paper.

But don't put your name on it. Once all of you have finished drawing, put the pictures in a pile, shuffle them, and then let everyone see each other's work. Can you guess who drew each picture?

People who go online become part of a digital community. That community is made of people like you. They are called **digital citizens**. Digital citizenship means following rules and treating others' creations with respect. One of the best ways to respect people online is by thanking them when you use their work. You should do this by writing the person's name down. Choose one of the pictures to show on an imaginary website. Ask your friends if that would be OK. Finally, give everyone their drawings back and have everyone sign their work. That way, you will know who to thank!

Social Media Safety

NUMBER OF PLAYERS 1

TIME NEEDED

15–20 minutes

You'll Need
- Pencil
- Drawing supplies
- Paper

ACTIVITY OVERVIEW

Today, technology brings everyone around the world closer together. People like to go on social media. It is important to know that you can't go on social media until you are at least thirteen years old. Popular social media tools are Instagram and Snapchat. People share photos, stories, or moods about their life. However, sometimes people share too much. How can someone tell when they've shared too much? Even though you can't go on social media until you're older, you can imagine what it would be like to share on social media. In this activity, you will think about sharing online.

INSTRUCTIONS

Trace your foot on a piece of paper. You can have your parents or a friend help you do this. Then, think about what you want the world to know about you. Draw pictures or write words inside your footprint. The drawings and words should say what things you would post on social media. What you write in the footprint is called a "digital footprint." Social media can be a fun place to tell your friends and family about activities you've done. However, be careful about what you post. The things you share online last forever.

Privacy and Sharing

NUMBER OF PLAYERS ⬤1

TIME NEEDED

15–20 minutes

ACTIVITY OVERVIEW

In a digital world, information shared online does not go away. It is forever. It is important to remember this whenever you post online. (Also remember that most sites need you to be thirteen years old to join and post.) It is also important to think about what information you share and how you share it. In this activity, you will think carefully about sharing information online.

INSTRUCTIONS

First, split a piece of paper into two parts by drawing a line down the middle. Then name one side "things to share." The other side should be "things to keep private." Then, make a list for both sides. One should list fun things to share online. The other should list things that are best kept private. As you work, remember that once you share something, you can't take it back! Does this make you change your mind about anything you have in the "share" column?

Glossary

ACROSTIC A kind of poem where one word is spelled vertically and other words describing an idea are written horizontally next to each letter of the main word.

CITATIONS Ways of giving someone thanks for their work. They usually involve writing down a person's name or the name of a newspaper article or book.

CODERS Another word for computer programmers.

COMPUTATIONAL THINKING A way of thinking where you break a big task into smaller tasks.

COMPUTER SCIENCE The study of computers and how they work.

DATA Information.

DIGITAL CITIZENS People who use computers to go online and post to social media or comment on websites.

DIGITAL CITIZENSHIP Belonging to the online community of digital citizens.

Find Out More

BOOKS

Lieberman, Suzy. *Teamwork*. Hugo the Happy Starfish. Self-Published: Happy Language Kids LLC, 2015.

Wainewright, Max. *How to Code: A Step-by-Step Guide to Computer Coding*. New York: Sterling Publishing, 2016.

WEBSITE

Kano

https://kano.me/articles/coding-for-kids

Coding company Kano's official website explores coding for kids.

VIDEO

Pair Programming

https://www.youtube.com/watch?v=vgkahOzFH2Q

Two female student programmers talk about working on a computer program together.

Index

Entries in **boldface** are glossary terms.

acrostic, 7, 20–21

citations, 24–25

coders (programmers), 4–5, 6, 8, 12, 20, 22

computational thinking, 4, 6–7, 8–9, 10, 12, 14, 16, 18, 20, 24

computer science, 10

data, 24

digital citizens, 25

digital citizenship, 5, 24–25, 26–27, 28–29

digital footprint, 27, 28–29

group activities, 6–7, 8–9, 14–15, 24–25

guessing, 12–13, 16–17

individual activities, 10–11, 12–13, 16–17, 18–19, 20–21, 22–23, 26–27, 28–29

limits, 7, 20–21

measuring, 13, 14–15, 17

planning, 16–17, 18

privacy, 26–27, 28–29

problem-solving, 4–5, 6–7, 8, 10–11, 14, 16–17, 18–19

reusing, 24–25

sharing, 25, 26–27, 28–29

social media, 26–27, 28–29

teamwork, 4–5, 6–7, 8–9, 10–11, 14–15, 22

thanking people, 22–23, 24–25

trial and error, 4, 13, 14–15, 16–17, 18–19

FELLOWSHIP OF CHRISTIAN ATHLETES

SERVING
PLAYBOOK

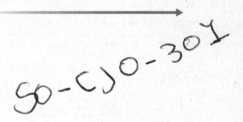

**TRUE CHAMPIONS TALK ABOUT
THE HEART AND SOUL IN SPORTS**

SO-CJO-30I

Revell

a division of Baker Publishing Group
Grand Rapids, Michigan

Published by Revell
a division of Baker Publishing Group
P.O. Box 6287, Grand Rapids, MI 49516-6287
www.revellbooks.com

Material adapted from *Serving*, published in 2008 by Regal Books.

ISBN 978-0-8007-2673-7

Printed in the United States of America

15 16 17 18 19 20 21   7 6 5 4 3 2

Contents

The Four Core   7

Introduction: *The Heart of Serving*   13

1. **Living a Paradox**   19

   Tony Dungy
   Winning Super Bowl Coach of the Indianapolis Colts

2. **Focused on Purpose**   41

   Kyle Korver
   NBA Shooting Guard

3. **Called to Love**   53

   Elana Meyers-Taylor
   Olympic Bobsled Silver Medalist

4. **True Leadership** 67

   Pat Williams
   Senior Vice President of the
   Orlando Magic

5. **Pride Fighter** 89

   Tim Tebow
   Former NFL Quarterback and Heisman
   Trophy Winner

6. **Open Hearts** 111

   Betsy King
   Former LPGA Golfer

   Thanks 131

   Impacting the World for Christ
   Through Sports 133

   FCA Competitor's Creed 135

   FCA Coach's Mandate 139

The Four Core

*Executive Vice President of
International Ministry, Fellowship
of Christian Athletes*

The NCAA Final Four tournament is an exciting sporting event. Even if you are not a person who likes basketball, it is awesome to watch March Madness as it narrows down sixty-four teams into four core teams. This makes me think about Fellowship of Christian Athlete's "Four Core"—not four core teams, but four core values.

Core values are simply the way you live and conduct yourself. They are your attitudes, beliefs and convictions. Values should be what you are, not what you want to become. The goal is to embody your values every step of the way.

Are your values just words, or do you actually live them out? Can others identify the values in your life without you telling them? Your values need to be a driving force that shapes the way you do life! Talk is cheap, but values are valuable.

When everything is stripped away, what is left? For FCA, it is integrity, serving, teamwork, and excellence. These Four Core are so powerful to me that I have made them my own personal values. So, I have to ask you, what are your values? What guides you? Let me share with you FCA's Four Core, which are even better than the Final Four!

Integrity

To have integrity means that you are committed to Christlike wholeness, both privately and publicly. Basically, it means to live without gaps. Proverbs 11:3 says that integrity should guide you, but that a double life will destroy you. You need to be transparent, authentic, honest, and trustworthy. You should be the same in all situations and not become someone different when the competition of the game begins. Integrity means to act the same when no one is looking as you do when all eyes are on you. It is not about being perfect, but, as a coach or athlete, you need to be the real deal.

Serving

In John 13:12–15, Jesus gives us the perfect example of serving when He washes the disciples' feet. He then commands the disciples to go and do unto others what

He has done to them. How many of your teammates' feet have you washed? Maybe not literally, but spiritually, do you have an attitude of serving just as if you were washing their feet in the locker room? You need to seek out the needs of others and be passionate about pursuing people who are needy. And, the last time I checked, everyone is needy.

Teamwork

Teamwork means to work together with others and express unity in Christ in all of your relationships. In Philippians 2:1–5, Paul encourages each of us to be one, united together in spirit and purpose. We all need to be on one team—not just the team we play on, but on God's Team! We need to equip, encourage, and empower one another. Do you celebrate and hurt together as teammates? You need to be arm-in-arm with others, locking up to-

gether to accomplish God's work. There should be no Lone Rangers.

Excellence

To pursue excellence means to honor and glorify God in everything you do. In Colossians 3:23–24, Paul writes, "whatever you do, work at it with all your heart, as working for the Lord, not for men." The "whatever" part is hard, because it means that everything you do must be done for God, not others. You need to pursue excellence in practice, in games, in schoolwork and in lifting weights. God deserves your best, not your leftovers.

It is tip-off time for the game of life. How will you be known?

Introduction

The Heart of Serving

Whatever happens, conduct your-
selves in a manner worthy of the
gospel of Christ.

Philippians 1:27 NIV

Lord Jesus, my prayer is to live and compete with integrity, serving, teamwork, and excellence. It is a high standard, but I know that with Your power and strength, it can happen. I want all my relationships to be known for things that are of You. Search my heart and reveal to me my values. I lay at the foot of the cross the values that do not honor You, and I ask for Your forgiveness. The values that bring You glory, I lay at the foot of the cross for Your anointing.

The Heart of Serving

As we dive into the core value of serving, we must realize that God calls everyone to serve. There is no one that is excluded from this value. It is not just for those who have the gift of serving or for those for whom it comes naturally. When we choose to serve others, we discover that

there is power in serving others—not natural power, but supernatural power. It is not about getting power, but about giving power.

Many people serve so that they can be served, but this is not the type of serving that pleases God. The ultimate purpose of serving is for God's glory. After we have served others, we should say, "God is good," not "I am good."

The purpose of serving is to lift up the name of Jesus. Rick Warren says, "We serve God by serving others. The world defines greatness in terms of power, possessions, prestige, and position. In our self-serving culture with its me-first mentality, acting like a servant is not a popular concept." When we serve, we represent to the world what Jesus looks like.

The heart of serving is to take every gift, skill, talent, and ability that God has given us and use it to serve others. That type of serving will stir the passion in our hearts. Each day, we should start

by asking ourselves, *Whom can I serve today?* Perhaps Samuel Chadwick nailed it best when he wrote, "Spirit-filled souls are ablaze for God. They love with a love that glows. They serve with a faith that kindles. They serve with a devotion that consumes."

When done right, serving is about love, not duty. When it is done out of love, joy is the byproduct of serving, not regret or guilt. Serving should come freely and not feel forced. It is an opportunity, not an obligation. We serve without thinking that we are going to get something back, because serving is about others, not self.

In Philippians, Paul challenges us to do nothing out of selfish ambition. We need to consider others better than ourselves, because self-denial is the core of serving. So, the tough question we need to ask ourselves is, *Am I serving or self-serving?* That is why serving is costly, not convenient. Sacrifice is always a key ingredient!

Additionally, we cannot serve with a critical or insecure heart. The more insecure we are, the harder it is for us to serve, because we will always want others to serve us and meet our own needs. Only people with a secure heart can serve. Serving is forged out of a heart that is yielded to Jesus, one whose identity is in Christ!

Bottom line: Serving is not an option. We need to be radical about serving others. Can you imagine the impact if thousands of Christians were to get passionate about serving their communities? Why shouldn't that revolution begin with us?

How to Use this Book

Serving Playbook takes an in-depth look at this core value and comes at it from six different angles as lived out by six different people. Their insights shed new light on this value and give us a model to follow.

You can read *Serving Playbook* individually or as part of a group. As part of a personal devotion time, you can gain insight as you read through each story and ponder the "Training Time" questions at the end. Mentors can also use this book in a discipleship relationship, using the "Training Time" questions to step up conversations to the next level. And small groups (huddles) can study the core value as a group to be prepared to sharpen each other with questions.

1

Living a Paradox

TONY DUNGY
*Winning Super Bowl Coach
of the Indianapolis Colts*

Let your light shine before men, so that they may see your good works and give glory to your Father in heaven.

Matthew 5:16

Setting an example is not the main means of influencing another, it is the only means.

Albert Einstein

One of the hardest obstacles for some people to overcome when it comes to accepting the Bible as infallible truth is the pervasive presence of paradox. The inclusion of these seemingly contradictory statements often plays tricks on the logical mind, even though the truth behind them can always be substantiated by neighboring Scriptures or by concepts revealed in more distant parts of God's Word.

Most of these paradoxical statements can be located in the four Gospels, where Jesus confounded the religious leaders of His time. For example, in Matthew 11:29–30, Jesus tells us that we can find rest in working for Him. In Matthew 19:30, He says that the "first will be last, and many who are last will be first" (NIV).

Another one of Christ's more prominent paradoxes can be found in Matthew 16:25, where Jesus tells His disciples, "For whoever wants to save his life will lose it, but whoever loses his life because of Me will find it."

But spiritual paradoxes don't just exist in the Bible. There are living, breathing examples of this concept that can be readily found in the world around us.

Take for instance Tony Dungy. During his time as head coach of the Indianapolis Colts, he consistently turned conventional wisdom on its head. Consider the fact that Dungy always got his players' attention without raising his voice or

swearing. He was also a highly successful NFL coach and an equally successful family man.

And then there's Dungy's curious belief that to be an effective leader, one must actually be a servant to those he is leading. Dungy, now back in the spotlight as an NFL analyst for NBC Sports, got this paradoxical idea from Matthew 20:26–27, where Jesus teaches that "whoever wants to become great among you must be your servant, and whoever wants to be first among you must be your slave."

"Ever since I've been in a leadership position, my focus has been the model of Christ as the servant-leader," Dungy says. "There are different ways to lead, but I've always felt that it's better if other people follow me because they want to follow, not because I've been put up there as the leader and they have to follow. To do that, you have to earn people's trust and their respect, and the way to do that is to show them you are there to help them.

As coaches, that what's our job is—not necessarily to win a championship, but to help all the players, everyone in the organization, do their job as well as they can. That really is serving."

In an age when players work tirelessly to gain the approval of their coaches in order to earn starting positions and playing time, Dungy was a rare breed. He didn't relish the role of leader as a means to attain self-gratification or a propped-up sense of respect. Instead, Dungy truly saw himself as a servant to his players and his coaching staff. His main objective was to make everyone around him better at what they do.

"To me, Christ's model really was the best," Dungy says. "I really tried to, number one, be a role model and serve my team spiritually. I wanted to teach them as much as I could about football and how to be better players; but I also wanted to help them be good people, do well in the community and do well after football. So

I tried to present those things to them so that they could see that football isn't the end of the road. Therefore, I was hopefully serving them as individuals, serving their families, and also serving them by giving everything I have to make them the best players they can be."

Former Colts linebacker Tyjuan Hagler is certainly a believer in Dungy's methods. Hagler, also a professing Christian, thoroughly enjoyed playing in Indianapolis where he was a member of the Dungy-led Super Bowl XLI championship team. He saw the serving nature of his coach even in the small things—such as Dungy's consistently laid-back demeanor and his approach to teaching through respectful personal interaction.

"I don't like it when coaches yell at me and cuss me out," Hagler says. "I like the coaches like him that just talk to you and break things down, like what you did wrong and what you need to do to correct it. I respect him so much for

his coaching style, and I've got to thank God for bringing me to that team and Coach Dungy because that's the kind of coaching I responded better to."

Dungy was exposed to the concept of serving at a very young age. In fact, he was raised by two parents who exemplified such a lifestyle through their strong commitment to education in Jackson, Michigan, where Dungy was born and raised. Dr. Wilbur and CleoMae Dungy set a standard for their son that was further solidified by other close family members.

"[My parents'] attitude toward their jobs was that they were really helping people learn," Dungy recalls. "My grandfather was a minister, and I had two uncles who were ministers. That was their chosen way of serving and helping people understand the gospel and really doing it for other people's benefit. So I think I got to see that very early on just by watching my family."

Dungy also learned early on that serving isn't some complicated or even scary process that includes traveling to third-world countries or forsaking one's dreams for a life dedicated to full-time ministry. Instead, he has always had a balanced view of what being a servant truly entails.

"When I think of serving, I think of using the talents that the Lord has given you to help other people," Dungy simply states. "We always talk about using our talents for a purpose, but if you use them to help other people, I really feel like you're a servant.

"I just feel like I have that responsibility to model serving to others," he adds. "Some of the volunteer work I do, the charity work, is very satisfying; but it's satisfying because you feel like you've helped some other people—whether it's visiting a prison or a jail, whether it's helping out with Big Brothers or a Boys and Girls Club by giving someone an ex-

ample. That part of it is important, and getting your satisfaction comes from feeling like you've helped someone, especially a young person."

That desire to help young people—especially young athletes—is a primary reason behind Dungy's lifelong support of Fellowship of Christian Athletes (FCA). He has seen time and again how one little spark can change another individual's outlook forever. Dungy believes that the ministry of FCA provides an invaluable opportunity for coaches to point young people toward Jesus. As far as Dungy is concerned, there is no better union than the one between athletics and ministry.

"I love the Bible, and the Bible really talks about how working for the Lord and athletics go hand in hand in a number of places," Dungy says. "Paul uses so many athletic metaphors because it's so fitting. It's hard work. It's not easy. You need determination. You have to be physically tough. You have to be mentally strong.

And that to me is the image that I get of us as Christians and how we should be working for the Lord."

Dungy has served as a mentor in numerous organizations, such as Big Brothers, the Boys and Girls Club of America, All Pro Dad and, of course, FCA. But it's that daily routine of teaching his players both football skills and life skills that he continues to find most rewarding. And from experience, he knows just how important that relationship can be over the length of an athlete's career.

"So many players that I coached," Dungy says, "when I asked them who the guiding force in their life was if they didn't have a dad, if they didn't have a mom who got you going, they all say it was a high-school coach or a junior-high teacher or someone in their life when they were growing up. It was a tremendous thing to be able to not only impact those players on the field in their sport but also impact them as people.

"Because of that responsibility of shaping players spiritually as well as athletically, I think it's so important that we as coaches feed ourselves spiritually. We all go to clinics. We all go to camps. We understand our sport. But we need to understand what God wants us to do and to stay focused in our life so that we can not only tell our players what to do, we can show them. I think that's so critical."

When Dungy shares his philosophy on mentoring as part of the coaching process, he's not just reading from the pages of the latest bestseller on leadership, and he's not bringing a belief that he conjured up over years of experience. Instead, Dungy brings to the table a tried-and-true method of relational leadership that was modeled over two thousand years ago by the ultimate servant-leader.

"Jesus had quite a few disciples, but there were twelve guys that He really poured Himself into," Dungy says. "Everything He did was to make those

guys the best team they could be. At times, that involved teaching. At times, it involved Him being the example. At times, it involved one-on-one talks. For me, it was the same thing. I wanted my players to know that I wasn't the one trying to be up front and get all the rewards of our business, but I was really there to make them the best team they could be. That involved working as hard as I could, spending hours studying the other team to get our game plans ready, and doing everything I could for them so that they could play well. But it's more than that. It was being involved, being there for them, being a sounding board for them and trying to help their families out. Anything that could help them get better at what they do, I was here to provide that."

And that brings us back to this mind-boggling concept of paradox. Dungy's desire to serve others as a means to draw attention to his faith appears to send a conflicting message. But he takes his cue

from Matthew 5:16, where Jesus says, "Let your light shine before men, so that they may see your good works." If you end the Scripture there, it obviously seems a bit odd that Jesus would encourage His followers to serve others just to get attention. That's why it's imperative to finish (and then digest) the rest of that verse, which goes on to say, "And give glory to your Father in heaven."

In other words, there is a greater purpose to serving than simply to help others. That is certainly a big part of the equation. God is, after all, a compassionate and caring God. But ultimately, we are to engage in a lifestyle of serving as a way to draw attention to God's mercy and grace and bring glory to His name. Even then, there is yet another purpose for serving that is often overlooked.

"I do think it's important for us to benefit other people, to help other people," Dungy says. "But I do think that in every station of life, we need role models. We,

as Christians, need to model Christ and to show our young people what life is all about. Life is not all about taking, getting, receiving, taking advantage of opportunities that are presented to you, but life is also helping."

Jesus Himself proved this concept to be true during His ministry on Earth. As He healed the sick, fed the hungry, set the captives free, and shared the message of eternal life with the masses that followed Him from town to town, Jesus did so knowing that His disciples were taking mental notes of everything He was doing.

"[Jesus] did some things in the course of His ministry strictly to show the disciples why He was here, what His mission was; and He said, 'Let this be an example to you,'" Dungy says. "He washed their feet so that they would understand what He was doing, why He was doing it, and what they were supposed to do as well. So I think that role modeling was an important part of His ministry."

Not only did Jesus model serving for His disciples, but He also modeled serving for every generation to follow. His actions were intended to set off a chain reaction of selfless living among those who have chosen to bear the name of Christ. And for Dungy, that meant being concerned with the physical and emotional needs of every athlete on the Colts' roster.

"It's a big part of it, to show your players that you're really there to make them better players," Dungy says. "I told them that all the time. That was our job as coaches. It was nothing more than to help them get better. Yes, there were some personal benefits that we got out of it; but really if we're in it for the personal benefits, we're in it for the wrong reasons. You're a coach to help your team and your players grow. When you see guys grow and you see players get better on the field—you see them mature and gain confidence and all those things—

that's where you get all of your satisfaction: from knowing that you have helped someone."

The light that shines before men through the witness of a servant like Dungy can't be contained by the walls of a football locker room. Jesus explains in Matthew 5:14 that "a city situated on a hill cannot be hidden"—and neither can the servant's light as it radiates the love of God to everyone within that individual's sphere of influence. Such is the case with the highly influential Coach Dungy.

"[Tony] lives out two great biblical commands—to love God and to love others," ESPN senior NFL analyst Chris Mortensen confirms. "There is no hypocrite in him. I can't say that about many people. I can't say that about me. . . . But every time I speak with Tony or I'm around him or I hear of other people's experiences with him, the more I want to be like him."

Despite the high praises that Dungy receives on a seemingly daily basis, his spirit of humility wards off any temptation to take even the shortest of ego trips. But he can't deny the joys that accompany a life of serving—especially when the fruits of his labor are born.

"For me, the biggest blessing comes down the road when someone says, 'Gee, that was really helpful to me,'" Dungy says. "It might not come right away. I know with the players, sometimes it comes twelve years later; and you're visiting with someone and they say, 'What happened in 1996 really made an impact on me, and here's how it helped.' There's no better feeling than that."

But according to Dungy, even more important than the blessings of serving is the call that every believer has received through the undeniable example of God's Son. "Christ said that [serving] was His mission," Dungy says. "That should tell us something."

Training Time

1. In what ways is Tony Dungy's life a living example of serving? Can you think of some other people, famous or not, who provide similar examples? What attributes do they possess and display? How do those people inspire you?

2. Who are some examples of serving in your life? How have they had an impact on you? How might others say that you are an example?

3. Read Matthew 5:16. What do you think Jesus meant when He said, "Let your light shine before men"? How do you think your good works can bring glory or attention to God?

4. Tony Dungy says, "Life is not all about taking, getting, receiving, taking advantage of opportunities that are presented to you, but life is also helping." Why do you think so many people in government, athlet-

ics, entertainment, and society tend to live the opposite of what Coach Dungy is suggesting?

5. What are some ways that you can be an example to your classmates, your teammates, your coworkers, your family members, or your friends?

journal

2

Focused on
Purpose

KYLE KORVER
NBA Shooting Guard

So we must not get tired of doing good, for we will reap at the proper time if we don't give up.

Galatians 6:9

The purpose of life is not to be happy. It is to be useful, to be honorable, to be compassionate, to have it make some difference that you have lived and lived well.

Ralph Waldo Emerson

Kyle Korver is arguably one of the greatest perimeter shooters to play in the NBA. The proof is in his staggering statistics. Korver is ranked in the top five for career three-point shooting percentage and ranked in the top fifteen for career three-point shots made. In 2014, he set an NBA record with 127 consecutive games with a made three-pointer, shattering Dana Barros' previous

record of 89 games. It took twelve seasons, but Korver reached another milestone when he was added to the 2015 Eastern Conference All-Star Team roster.

Being a long-range sharp shooter requires precision, and precision requires focus—focus on the rim and focus on the fundamentals.

Ironically, Korver doesn't consider himself to be one of the most athletic players on the floor. That's why he's always worked harder to get the most out of his ability.

"People ask me what my goal is in basketball," Korver says. "I just want to squeeze every ounce of potential that I have out of me. That means doing things the right way and having to make some tough decisions and maybe choosing a more difficult path. But in the end, there's a satisfaction in knowing I went through all of that to achieve my goals."

Korver's path to the NBA didn't travel through one of the typical collegiate

powerhouse programs. Instead, he stayed closed to his home in Pella, Iowa, and played for Creighton University, just three hours to the west in Omaha, Nebraska. While there, his work ethic paid significant dividends. Korver was a two-time Missouri Valley Conference Player of the Year and a second-team All-American.

"I'd stay up late to shoot around in the gym or stay late after practice," Korver recalls. "It wasn't to impress the coach. It wasn't to be in good favor with him. I didn't just do it when he was around so he could hear the ball bouncing in the gym. I went because I loved it, and because it was fun and there was a joy in it."

That spirit of joy has carried over into Korver's NBA career, where he believes God has given him a platform to carry out a greater purpose. Part of that purpose is to demonstrate Christ's love to those around him and to those who might be watching him from a distance. And ultimately, Korver believes that his purpose

is built on a foundation of serving others. It's a lesson he learned from two very influential men in his life.

"My Grandpa Harold Korver is the pastor of Emmanuel Reformed Church in Paramount, California," Korver says. "He's led that large congregation for about forty years now. As a pastor, he's had a lot of big goals for his church. But one thing he told was this: 'There were a thousand people in the church, but I had five sons. And my primary focus was on them.' Now that he's almost eighty years old, he can look at those five sons that he poured most of his energy into, and he can see all of the fruit that they've produced. That was so much more than he could have done on his own. So instead of going every different direction, he focused on the important things—his five sons."

That act of putting family first directly led to Korver's father, Kevin Korver, going into the ministry as well and filling the role of senior pastor at Third Reformed

Church in Pella. Before moving to Iowa, Korver spent his younger days in Paramount, where he observed his father start a program called, "Looking Good." The program helped clean up neighborhoods and turned a dying town into a thriving city.

When Korver isn't focused on draining three-point shots from most any spot behind the arc, he is finding ways to carry on his family's tradition of helping others in need. It all began in Philadelphia, where his career started with the 76ers in 2003. Korver joined a Bible study group that met on the north side of town. Over time, he connected with the young people living there and started thinking about ways he could help improve their struggling community. From there, he created the Kyle Korver Foundation and got more involved through public education and after-school programs.

When he was traded to the Utah Jazz during the 2008 season, Korver continued

his work in Philadelphia, but also brought that same mentality of serving to Salt Lake City. Two and a half years later, he landed in Chicago, where he played two seasons and dove into the city's most impoverished precincts. After two years with the Bulls, Korver found his way to the Atlanta Hawks and discovered yet another place where he could serve those in need.

Along the way, Korver also made a commitment to serving in Omaha where he played collegiately at Creighton, and as far away as Africa, where he has participated in humanitarian work.

"I believe change is possible," Korver says. "Change comes through authentic relationships, athletic opportunities, academic support, talent development and Christian guidance. I'm committed to creating and sustaining those opportunities. I want to show love, give love and to help others do the same."

But staying focused on his purpose isn't always easy. That's why he works

diligently to keep his eyes fixed on his calling and avoid getting distracted. For Korver, it's all about keeping things simple.

"In today's world, there's so much stuff going on and there are so many possibilities," he says. "It's easy to get sidetracked, but I just have to focus on what's important and do the simple things well."

Korver also says it's important to embrace the concept of accountability.

"As humans we're only so strong," he adds. "If you put yourself in enough bad situations, you will fail eventually. That's the lesson I've learned over a lot of years of making good decisions and making mistakes. That's why you need to find good people that will build you up and not tear you down. You've got to surround yourself with people that will help keep you on the right path."

Even though Korver has spent many years in the NBA and been paid well for his unique skills, he makes sure not to let material possessions impact his ability to

serve. On the contrary, Korver sees those things as gifts to be given away.

"I've come to grips with the fact that nothing is owned," he says. "Are you 100 percent willing to admit that everything you have is loaned from God? When you come to that conclusion, then you're going to be okay with whatever He has for you to do."

And that's what serving others is really all about—trust in God. It is the one thing that allows us to focus on our true purpose in life.

"It's not always the easy road," Korver says. "But it comes down to whether or not you trust that God has a plan for you. When you pray, expect the unexpected. God works things out in ways that we don't always expect. He opens the doors that He wants us to walk through. God will put people in our paths that we can serve and help see how much He loves them. That is what all of us as Christians should be focused on."

Training Time

1. What would you say is your purpose in life? Is it just one purpose or are there many purposes to which you have been called? Explain.

2. How do you think that serving others fits into the concept of purpose?

3. What are some things that can distract you from fulfilling your purpose? How often do you find yourself sidetracked?

4. Korver talks about four things that keep him focused on the purpose of serving others: simplicity, accountability, generosity, and trust. With which of those things do you feel comfortable? With which of those things do you struggle?

5. What attitudes and practices do you need to change in order to help you stay focused on your purpose? How do you think that sticking to that purpose and serving others will impact your life?

journal

3

Called to Love

ELANA MEYERS-TAYLOR
Olympic Bobsled Silver Medalist

Love your neighbor as yourself.
Matthew 22:39

We love those whom we serve.
Richard Paul Evans

Elana Meyers-Taylor was born into an Episcopalian family that later became Lutheran. More recently, she was baptized in a Baptist church. She's also been known to attend nondenominational services from time to time. So Meyers-Taylor really isn't sure how to label her Christian faith.

But the two-time Olympian and 2010 bronze medalist does know that she is first and foremost a follower of Christ. For Meyers-Taylor, that means doing things a little differently within the highly competitive sport of bobsled.

"The Lord calls us to love everybody," she says. "Every day it's a challenge. Within this sport, I'm called to love everybody. That means that every single German or Canadian that I want to beat, I still have to love."

Meyers-Taylor's faith journey hasn't been her only experience with diversity. In fact, her sports career has taken her down an equally unusual path. Meyers-Taylor grew up in Douglasville, Georgia, where her father Eddie Meyers played for the nearby Atlanta Falcons. At the age of nine, she started playing softball and quickly began cultivating dreams of becoming an Olympian.

"I didn't know what that meant at the time," Meyers-Taylor admits. "But I thought it might be in a warm summer sport like softball. I played a variety of sports growing up—basketball, soccer, and track. I really didn't care. I just wanted to be an Olympian."

Meyers-Taylor played well enough to earn a softball scholarship from George Washington University. From there, she played professionally for the Mid-Michigan Ice. She even had a couple of tryouts with the US Olympic Team, one of which she describes as "the worst try-out in the history of tryouts."

"It was that bad," Meyers-Taylor recalls. "I totally bombed it and thought my chances of being an Olympian were over."

Nothing could be further from the truth. After her parents watched bobsled-ding on television in 2002, they encouraged her to give it a try. Five years later, she retired from softball and went to Lake Placid, New York, for a tryout with Team USA. She's been sliding down ice-paved tracks across the world ever since. Within two years, she had won her first world championship medal with a silver performance (with teammate Shauna Roh-bock) at the 2009 FIBT event in Lake Placid. Then, she added an Olympic

bronze medal (with teammate Erin Pac) to her trophy case at the 2010 Vancouver Games. Meyers-Taylor's skyrocketing success was a textbook example of how bobsledding stars are made, not born.

"No one really grows up competing in the bobsled," she explains. "You have to be sixteen years old before you can even drive one. And there are really only two places in the country where you can bobsled—Park City, Utah, and Lake Placid, New York. There's not really much of an opportunity for a girl from Georgia like me to grow up bobsledding. That's what I love about the sport. It gives athletes from very diverse backgrounds the opportunity to compete at an elite international level."

Just like in her athletic career, Meyers-Taylor has been growing in her faith at an equally steady pace. She married her coach and fellow bobsled competitor Nic Taylor in 2014 and together they are learning what it means to serve like Jesus and compete in a manner that pleases God.

"That means doing things that might not necessarily be seen as giving me a competitive advantage but instead doing what God would want me to do," Meyers-Taylor explains. "As Christians, we're asked to give. In my sport, if someone needs equipment or help with something, regardless of who they are as a competitor, I'm called to help them for a higher purpose. It's not easy. It's very hard to love everyone. It requires us to act outside of the flesh. God doesn't call us to serve just when it's easy. That's why we need to rely on His strength. That's when His glory is revealed."

For all Christians, that call can be discovered in a conversation that Jesus had with some of the religious leaders of His time. The Pharisees were trying to trap Him into giving a provocative answer that might expose Him as a fraud, but instead Jesus reduced the entire sum of rabbinical law into two simple commandments.

"And one of them, an expert in the law, asked a question to test Him. 'Teacher,

which command in the law is the greatest?' He said to him, 'Love the Lord your
God with all your heart, with all your
soul, and with all your mind. This is the
greatest and most important command.
The second is like it: Love your neighbor
as yourself'" (Matt. 22:35-39).

Both commands involve a call to love.
The first is to love God. The second is to
love others. And when we truly love God,
loving others is something that should
naturally take place.

Meyers-Taylor had plenty of opportunity to walk out the principle of
serving others in love as she aimed for
a second shot at the Olympics. She won
back-to-back gold medals at the World
Championships in the mixed team competition and then won the silver medal
(with teammate Lauryn Williams) at the
2014 Olympics in Sochi. Throughout the
experience, she did her best to portray
a servant's heart and a desire to glorify
God above it all.

"I'm a representative of something that's greater than myself," Meyers-Taylor says. "When you see me out there on the track, I'm not just representing myself or my country, I'm representing Christ and what He's done through me. I have a responsibility to show His love and show others what He's done for me. It's also freed me up. I want to be a champion. I want to win gold medals. All of these things can be overwhelming. But regardless of whether I win or never compete again, I just have to trust that God has a plan for my life and know that I'm called to be His representative through the sport and outside of the sport."

Meyers-Taylor hasn't been alone in her journey. She is thankful for many Christian teammates who have modeled serving to each other along the way. The men's and women's bobsled teams routinely hold Bible studies while training and traveling. Meyers-Taylor says there is emotional and spiritual help shared amongst the group on a daily basis.

"It's awesome to be able to share your struggles as an athlete with other Christian athletes," she says. "That's one of the coolest things about sports ministry. We can share these common experiences with other Christians. Having Lolo Jones as a teammate, for example, has been great. I went through a tough week during the season leading up to the 2014 Olympics, and she sent me some scriptures. It really helped remind me why I was here. And it's not just the US teams, but there are also many believers from the international community including several from the Canadian team. We hope to grow Christianity throughout our sport."

In that sense, Meyers-Taylor has experienced what it feels like to be a part of the body of Christ outside of the traditional church setting. She has also learned firsthand the apostles' teachings about love and serving that were taught to the early Christians. These principles remain relevant today.

"Therefore, as we have opportunity, we must work for the good of all, especially for those who belong to the household of faith" (Gal. 6:10).

Meyers-Taylor adds that her marriage to Nic Taylor offers one of the most beautiful examples of serving. "He serves me and those around him because of his love for Christ," she says.

Being an Olympian is "one of the greatest honors" that Meyers-Taylor can ever imagine receiving. Wearing USA on her back gives her a sense of accomplishment that can't be easily described. But the opportunity to serve her teammates and her opponents is the biggest blessing of all.

"I'm here for a higher purpose, and it's not just to win medals," Meyers-Taylor says. "Winning is great and hopefully it gives me a platform to spread His love and to share His Word, but at the end of the day, I'm called to do what He wants me to do. There's a reason that God has me in the sport, and it's all about serv-

ing His purpose. That means loving and serving others."

Training Time

1. In what ways do you think serving others and love are connected?
2. Read Matthew 22:35-39. Why do you think Jesus said that loving God and loving others are the two greatest commandments?
3. Is it possible to serve others without love? Why or why not?
4. When do you find it easiest to serve others? When do you find it most difficult?
5. What are some things that you can do today that will help you better fulfill God's call to love and serve others?

4

True Leadership

PAT WILLIAMS

*Senior Vice President of
the Orlando Magic*

Whoever wants to become great among you must be your servant, and whoever wants to be first among you must be your slave; just as the Son of Man did not come to be served, but to serve, and to give His life—a ransom for many.

Matthew 20:26–28

Everybody can be great . . . because anybody can serve.

Dr. Martin Luther King, Jr.

From his study of leadership, Pat Williams is convinced that there are seven sides to being an effective leader. The first is vision, or the ability to see down the road. Next is a gift for communicating that vision. Williams also says that people skills are an important leadership trait.

This includes a true heart for people and a genuine interest in their lives. The next three qualifications are character, competence, and boldness.

As the senior vice president of the NBA's Orlando Magic, Williams certainly has built a lengthy career by displaying a high level of acumen in those six areas.

But it's the seventh characteristic that he says makes the better-than-average leader a great leader.

"There are many six-sided leaders out there, and they are doing a good job," Williams says. "But to be a leader for the ages—one who will never be forgotten, a leader who will go down in the history books—the seventh side of leadership must be there. That is called a servant's heart, though I like the verb form better— a serving heart. When a man or woman in leadership has a serving heart, that person will always be remembered."

Over the course of history, there have been many seven-sided leaders. Some

notable figures that immediately cross Williams' mind include the Old Testament hero Joseph, along with such other historical figures as William Wilberforce, Dr. David Livingstone, Dr. Albert Schweitzer, Ghandi, Mother Teresa, Dr. Martin Luther King, Jr., President Ronald Reagan, Billy Graham, John Wooden, and Senator Robert Kennedy.

And then there's R. E. Littlejohn.

If you've never heard of Littlejohn, don't feel bad. Williams didn't know who he was either until 1965, when he went to work for the Philadelphia Phillies' farm club in Spartanburg, South Carolina, a team owned by Littlejohn. As a budding executive and rookie general manager, Williams immediately became enamored with the wealthy businessman who made his money in oil transportation.

Previously, Williams (a seven-year Army veteran) had spent two years as a minor-league catcher with the Phillies, preceded by a successful stint playing

college baseball at Wake Forest, where he was part of the 1962 Atlantic Coast Conference Championship team and was later inducted into the Wake Forest Sports Hall of Fame.

Despite the densely compacted life experience Williams brought to Spartanburg, it was nothing compared to the invaluable lessons he would learn from Littlejohn— his first true leadership mentor.

"Mr. Littlejohn had an enormous impact on me," Williams recalls. "He modeled servant leadership in front of me every day. He was wealthy and successful, but you never would have known it. People gravitated to him. He had a marvelous quality called wisdom, and people sought out that wisdom. He had a gentle, loving spirit. He loved the Lord and genuinely cared for people and put other people first. I just saw him modeling serving leadership. It left a huge impression on me."

In late February 1968, Williams committed his life to Christ at the age of

twenty-seven. Shortly thereafter, his career would take a trip on a fast track to success that included earning a master's degree at Indiana University and a doctorate from Flagler University. Williams was also eventually inducted into the Sports Hall of Fame in Delaware, the state in which he was raised.

Yet the faith he embraced—thanks to Littlejohn's example—helped him come to terms with the true meaning of life. And the "enormous change" that Williams experienced that day allowed him to see things from a completely different perspective.

"Up to that point, everything had been about me," he admits. "Then I realized that once Christ comes into your life, it's others first. That's how He lived His life, and that's the model He left for us. So I think at that point you really begin to change in your priorities."

After his stint within the Phillies' organization, Williams spent the next three

years doing similar work with the Minnesota Twins. Then, in 1968, he made the move to the NBA, where he's been ever since. Williams' stops have included Chicago, Atlanta, and Philadelphia, where he worked with the 1983 World Champion 76ers.

In 1987, he cofounded the Orlando Magic and helped lead them to the NBA finals in 1995. The following year, a prominent national magazine named Williams one of the fifty most influential people in NBA history. Perhaps that honor had something to do with the fact that twenty-three of his teams have made the playoffs and five of them have reached the finals.

Williams has also been involved in high-profile trades that involved the likes of Pete Maravich, Julius Erving, Moses Malone, and Penny Hardaway. He has also been a part of staffs that have drafted Charles Barkley, Shaquille O'Neal, Maurice Cheeks, Andrew Toney, Darryl Hawkins,

and Dwight Howard. Williams gave several prominent coaches—including Chuck Daly and Matt Guokas—their first coaching positions, and twelve of his former players have become head coaches while seventeen former players have become assistant coaches.

Beyond his success in the sports world, Williams has also become known as one of the nation's most popular motivational speakers and authors. But perhaps even more impressive is his active lifestyle, which boasts weight training and running. In fact, he has completed thirty-eight marathons over the past decade, including ten successful attempts at the Boston Marathon. On top of that, Williams participates in a Major League Baseball fantasy camp where he has caught for such Hall of Fame pitchers as Bob Gibson, Gaylord Perry, Tom Seaver, and Phil Niekro.

Yet nothing speaks to Williams' success quite like his role as a devoted husband

and father. He says it was that weighty responsibility that vastly increased his knowledge of serving.

"After I became a father was another huge turning point," Williams says. "Our family kept growing and growing and growing, and we ended up with nineteen children. I certainly learned in that world that you're constantly in a serving position. Now it's starting again with the grandchildren."

Of Williams' nineteen children, fourteen are adopted from four countries. While they are now all adults, there was one point in the family's fascinating history during which sixteen of the children were teenagers at the same time. This storybook angle has drawn attention from such national publications as *Sports Illustrated, Reader's Digest, Good Housekeeping* and the *Wall Street Journal*.

Williams has also learned about serving leadership by teaching an adult Sunday school class at First Baptist Church of

Orlando. He also says that his longtime partnership with Fellowship of Christian Athletes has been another integral part of his public life. While in Philadelphia, he established the local FCA chapter there during the 1968–69 season. When he moved to Chicago, he helped facilitate the FCA's burgeoning work there. Upon moving to Atlanta, Williams plugged into a preexisting FCA chapter before spending another twelve years with the 76ers, where he remained a key player in the organization's growth.

"Over the last forty years, many of the most rewarding experiences have been with the Fellowship of Christian Athletes," Williams says. "FCA involvement over the past four decades has probably been as fulfilling to me as anything that I've done while serving the body of Christ."

Williams says other educational opportunities have come from spending significant time with some modern ex-

amples of the serving leader. Legendary college basketball coach John Wooden and Orlando Magic ownership chairman Rich DeVos are two men in particular that Williams cites for their exemplary public and private service. In fact, he was so inspired by their examples, he wrote books about both men.

To this day, Coach Wooden—who coached the UCLA Bruins to an unprecedented ten consecutive NCAA titles—continues to amaze Williams. "John Wooden was the most successful coach of all time," he states. "He's set records that will never be touched. But Coach Wooden was a servant. He had a caring heart. He had a great love for other people, and he was never too busy for anybody. He was never too important for anybody. It was a beautiful thing to watch."

Another one of Williams's favorite examples of serving leadership is the world-famous evangelist Billy Graham. He has been privileged to speak at two

of Graham's crusades but has been even more blessed to see firsthand what kind of selfless humility it takes to truly have a servant's heart.

"I do a radio show in Orlando every week, and I once interviewed Ruth Graham, who is Billy Graham's youngest daughter," Williams recalls. "She had just written a book, and I was interviewing her about the book. Toward the end of the show I asked her just to reflect on her famous father. I asked Ruth to share some insight into her dad and why he was unique. Ruth Graham, in that wonderful North Carolina drawl, said, 'My daddy knows who he is—a flawed human being. In Daddy's mind, he's still just a farm boy from North Carolina.' And I thought that just captured it beautifully."

His impression of Graham was solidified even further when he traveled to Charlotte, North Carolina, where he was able to visit the Billy Graham Library and grounds, which were opened

to celebrate the minister's storied life. "You go through the barn and his boy-hood home," Williams describes. "Here's probably as famous an American as we've ever had in the past 100 years, and yet he just views himself as a country preacher from Charlotte. I like that quality very much. That truly appeals to me."

As impressive as Williams' list of mentors might be, in his opinion there is only one person who can be described as "the epitome of the serving leader." Williams is especially struck by the simple instruction and humility expressed by Jesus in Matthew 20:26–28. Yet even Williams' closest friends and confidantes had a hard time grasping this particular teaching that flies in the face of conventional wisdom and challenges human nature's deeply ingrained selfishness.

"Jesus had a very interesting philosophy," Williams says. "This is my version of the Scriptures, but basically He said to His disciples, 'You want to be great? Want

to get to the top? Want to be number one? I'll tell you how. Go out and serve other people.' I can just imagine how shocked they were when they heard that, because they were probably no different than anybody today. 'That's not what it says in this motivational book I'm reading, Jesus.' But that was His approach."

The ultimate example of Jesus's serving heart can be found in Matthew 26 (see also Mark 14 and Luke 22), in which Jesus went to a place called Gethsemane to pray with His disciples. He knew that the time of His death was near. In those moments, Jesus struggled with His humanity like never before. He cried out, "My Father! If it is possible, let this cup pass from Me. Yet not as I will, but as You will" (Matt. 26:39).

Even after enduring grueling and torturous experiences on the way to His crucifixion, Jesus still remained true to His serving spirit as He hung from the cross. In Luke 23:34, He prayed, "Father,

forgive them, because they do not know what they are doing."

Jesus's contrite, forgiving spirit stands in stark contrast to the cutthroat leadership that is typical of the management style often found in modern-day corporate America. Williams, however, believes that the current corporate philosophy is slowly but surely being phased out in exchange for the biblical alternative.

"So much of the time we're presented with leadership being a dominant force, overwhelming people or browbeating them or intimidating them," Williams says. "But I don't really think that's leadership. I think that's called assault and battery. I would suggest that the days of Attila the Hun leadership are over, as are the General Patton days. They're gone. And as leaders, we've got to avoid the temptation to adapt that style, because in the long run it demeans people and degrades people."

Williams says that leaders who feel the need to use domination and intimidation

in order to get others to follow them are usually bound by pride and selfishness. Sometimes that attitude is actually born out of the individual's struggle with self-worth and inferiority. Other times, it simply boils down to entitlement issues that infiltrate the soul like a ravenous cancer.

"We're always battling that," Williams says. "So many men and women, when they get promoted into a leadership position—they become the head coach or they become the athletic director or they become the CEO or the high-school principal—so many cannot handle an overflowing cup. They begin to inhale all of this stuff. And let's face it, with leadership there are some good things. There are some perks. Leaders get parking privileges and golf-club memberships and executive washroom keys and some really good stuff. But that good stuff has ruined more leaders than anything else. When we really begin to think that by divine right, this is all mine, that's the be-

ginning of the end. Any sense of a humble spirit is obliterated."

The Bible is clear about what happens to leaders (or anyone for that matter) who allow selfishness and pride to control their actions. Proverbs 16:18 tells us that "pride comes before destruction, and an arrogant spirit before a fall." Isaiah 2:11 prophecies that "human pride will be humbled, and the loftiness of men will be brought low."

Yet those seeking to be serving leaders can find solace in truths found in passages such as Proverbs 11:2, which suggests that "when pride comes, disgrace follows, but with humility comes wisdom." And along with that wisdom, the recognition of those golden opportunities to serve others can be much more easily found.

"At the end of the day, that's really what you'll be remembered for—what you contributed to other people's lives," Williams says. "That triggers my speaking and my writing. Every time I write a book or de-

liver a message, I want it to make a difference in people's lives. To get feedback later, you can't put a price tag on that. It's still the most uplifting experience I get in life."

Training Time

1. Pat Williams names seven keys to successful leadership. Name some people (living or dead, famous or not famous) who you think embody the qualities of a great leader. Which of those individuals would you say exhibit signs of the serving leader?

2. Read Matthew 20:20–28. In this story, how did James and John (and their mother) perceive the benefits of being a leader? How did Jesus's teaching on leadership contrast in comparison?

3. Read Matthew 26:39. Can you describe a time when you wanted God to pass the cup of responsibility to someone else? How did you gather

the strength to carry on with God's will for your life? What was the end result of that sacrifice?

4. Read Proverbs 16:18. What does this Scripture tell you about people who allow pride to keep them from a life of service? Can you describe some times in which your pride caused you to fall?

5. Read Proverbs 11:2. What benefit can be found for those who choose humility over pride? In what ways might wisdom help you to become a better leader? How can wisdom lead you to more opportunities for serving?

5

Pride Fighter

TIM TEBOW
Former NFL Quarterback and
Heisman Trophy Winner

Make your own attitude that of Christ Jesus, who, existing in the form of God, did not consider equality with God as something to be used for His own advantage. Instead He emptied Himself by assuming the form of a slave, taking on the likeness of men. And when He had come as a man in His external form, He humbled Himself by becoming obedient to the point of death—even to death on a cross.

Philippians 2:5–8

He that is proud eats up himself: pride is his own glass, his own trumpet, his own chronicle; and whatever praiseth itself but in the deed, devours the deed in the praise.

William Shakespeare

Tim Tebow, the 2007 Heisman Trophy winner and member of the 2006–07 National Championship Florida Gators, wasn't supposed to be a superstar quarterback. In fact, if his mother, Pam Tebow's, doctors would have had their way, his birth would have been permanently postponed.

In early 1987, Pam and her husband, Bob, were serving as missionaries in the Philippines. Pam was pregnant with Tim when she contracted amoebic dysentery—an intestinal infection caused by the presence of parasites in food or drink. Because of the strong possibility that the drugs she needed to combat the infection would endanger the unborn child, Pam's doctors strongly suggested that she have an abortion. After all, in their opinion, if the baby survived, it would very likely suffer from severe disabilities.

Every negative report was proven wrong on August 14, when a perfectly healthy boy was welcomed into the world. Tebow lived

in the Philippines with his family until he was three years old, but his unusual life was just beginning. In Jacksonville, Florida, he and his four siblings were all home-schooled by their mother, despite the fact that the practice was very uncommon at the time.

"I was the youngest, so for me it was pretty normal being home-schooled," Tebow says. "But when my parents starting home-schooling, it was an odd thing. No one really knew about it. They didn't always get praise for doing it, and some people frowned upon it. But my parents figured, 'Hey, there are some things we want our children to learn that are more important than academics.' It's not that they weren't stressing academics, which they were, but they were emphasizing more biblical things and character more than anything else. That's why my parents chose to home-school—so that we would learn to praise God and have character before learning our ABCs or how to

add. I'm thankful to my parents for doing that and instilling those things into me and my siblings."

One of the persistent criticisms against home-schooling has been the lack of extracurricular activities available to students not attending traditional public or private institutions. But in Florida, that changed in 1996 when legislation was passed allowing home-schooled students the opportunity to participate in local high school sports and other competitive activities.

Tebow was showing signs of athleticism, and the new law allowed him to play football at Trinity Christian Academy in Jacksonville, where he was a linebacker. But his desire to play quarterback in a passing offense caused him to search out other options. That search led him to Nease High School in Ponte Vedra Beach, where he and his mother moved into an apartment in the same county to gain eligibility. By his junior season, Tebow was

on every major college's recruiting list. His status was solidified when as a senior he led his team to the state title. He was also named to the prestigious All-State team. Tebow's exploits as a home-school prodigy eventually led advocates in the neighboring state of Alabama to create the Tim Tebow Bill, which would give its home-school athletes the same rights to compete on local high school sports teams.

When others try to heap praise on Tebow for the inspiration he has provided to so many people at such a young age, he is quick to give credit to his serving-minded parents, who diligently taught him about Jesus. But ultimately, Tebow says, he had to come to that life-changing decision on his own.

"I was blessed to grow up in a Christian home," he says. "We always went to church every Sunday, but it never really clicked for me until a few years down the road. I realized when I was still pretty young that even though I was a pretty

good person, I was a sinner too. Maybe I wasn't doing things that were bad in the eyes of the world, but I was still a sinner, and I needed a Savior. I realized that Christ died on the cross for my sins, and if I put my trust in Him, I'd have eternal life in heaven. I knew I needed that. I needed a Savior, and Jesus Christ was knocking on the door of my heart. So I received Him into my heart, and He's there with me today."

When it came time for Tebow to choose where to play college football, his faith was a strong component in the decision-making process. He eventually chose the tradition-rich University of Florida, which touted the 1996 National Championship and numerous NFL alumni, including Jack Youngblood, Cris Collinsworth, Emmitt Smith, Ike Hilliard, and Jevon Kearse, as well as Heisman Trophy winners Steve Spurrier and Danny Wuerffel.

His choice paid off almost immediately. As a freshman, he played a significant

part in the Gators' second BCS National Championship team during the 2006–07 campaign. Although Tebow was a backup quarterback to senior Chris Leak, he made major contributions as a dual-threat option and was called upon regularly in several key moments—including two touchdown passes and a rushing touchdown against Southeastern Conference opponent LSU and a touchdown pass and a rushing touchdown against Ohio State in the 2007 BCS National Championship game.

Tebow took the reins as quarterback as a sophomore in 2007 and proceeded to break multiple SEC and NCAA records. He became the first NCAA player to rush for twenty touchdowns and pass for twenty touchdowns in the same season. Tebow's ability to run and throw at equally high levels of proficiency earned him numerous accolades, including the Maxwell Award, the Davey O'Brien Award, and consensus First Team All-American honors.

He topped off his second season by becoming the first sophomore to win the prestigious Heisman Trophy, generally recognized as the ultimate prize in all of college football. Yet amazingly, Tebow has done his best to deflect much of the praise and redirect it elsewhere.

"I am not out there playing for myself," Tebow says. "I love the game, but I am playing for the Lord Jesus Christ. I am going out there and loving the game and giving everything I have 100 percent and hoping that they can see the love of Christ through me."

Some might assume that Tebow's humility has more to do with his laid-back personality or perhaps his humble beginnings in a missionary family. But there's so much more to his selfless style of leadership than meets the eye. In fact, Tebow looks at his role as a high-profile quarterback the same as any other position in life.

"I think anything can be a ministry, especially football, because you have a

platform," Tebow says. "You have 100 guys in the locker room with you every day. But more importantly than that, you have 1,000 kids looking up to you and a lot of people all across the country— you have the opportunity and platform to share with them, and to not take advantage of that would be a big mistake."

According to the University of Florida media relations department, Tebow received more than 200 requests for appearances and speaking engagements during his time on campus. Those inquiries came from a diverse list of organizations including churches, youth ministries, schools, and civic groups across the southeastern United States. Tebow credits Fellowship of Christian Athletes for much of his current understanding of what ministry looks like. He attended FCA events with his father and brothers as a five year old and has been involved ever since.

Even with such a solid supporting cast of family members and spiritual mentors,

Tebow says playing football on such a large platform presents its challenges. Thankfully, the wisdom that has been imparted into his life thus far provides an escape from the temptation of letting pride, self-importance and out-of-whack priorities take control.

"It's tough," Tebow admits. "You love a game like football. You love to play it. You love everything about it. It's tough once you've done it for so long to not let it become the number one thing in your life, not to let that become your god. You always have to realize that there are more important things than playing football or winning games or throwing a touchdown pass. It's more about how you're treating people and your relationship with Jesus Christ. Are you giving Him the honor and glory for everything? It takes staying in His Word and staying humble and realizing that there are things that are more important than football. I think that's the number one thing for me."

Tebow has also benefited from the example of boldness, courage, strength, and humility that his father has set for him. Having those attributes engrained into his heart, mind, and soul has given him a unique understanding of the difficult concept of serving.

"To me, serving means putting others' needs in front of your needs," Tebow says. "It's doing what you can to take care of other people before you focus on your own wants and needs. I learned the biblical principles of serving when I was very young, especially seeing how my parents have given of their time, life, and money to serve others around them."

Although Tebow was only three years old when he and his family moved back to Florida from the Philippines, he has been privileged to make several trips back to the heavily populated islands located in Southeast Asia. The experience has been both positive and educational.

"Meeting all of those different people who have nothing and are poor gave me an appreciation for what my family and I have," Tebow says. "It provided me with the perspective of taking nothing for granted. It also allowed me to see the effect that I could have on those people. For some, the belief in Christ is all that they have and is much more important than money or material possessions."

Tebow believes that his experience has also helped him to not get caught up in all the stress that is involved in being a leading college quarterback. "Going to the Philippines with my dad and being at the orphanage and hanging out with the kids help keep me from getting too wrapped up in what's going to happen on fourth down," Tebow says. "Instead, it lets me realize how much of a blessing it is to have the athletic ability to go out there and play football. That takes a lot of pressure off. It lets you go out there and enjoy playing and have fun."

Off the field, Tebow has quickly earned the reputation of having an eager willingness to serve the community, though, he admits, he must constantly be on the lookout for the enemies of serving, which include personal ambition and pride. "I think pride is an issue for everybody," Tebow says. "It is always an issue for everybody. You have to stay humble and realize that God gave you your abilities, and He can take them away at any time. You just have to be thankful for them and try to use the talents that God gave you to influence as many people as you can."

Long before Tebow was a Heisman Trophy winner and an All-American, his ministry-focused parents laid a solid foundation that has since helped keep his pride in check. "It's funny, but when I was very young in t-ball and stuff, my parents would never let me tell anyone how many home runs I hit or how many touchdowns I scored," he recalls. "They would never let me say it until the other person would

ask me. So when I was five or six or seven, I'd always want to be like, 'I just hit three home runs,' but I was never allowed to tell them until they asked me. That was a lesson I learned when I was really young. God blessed me with athletic ability, and that can be taken away in an instant. So I've just been thankful for it and never let myself get too proud. Just because you play football doesn't make you any more special than anybody else.

"I like to think that I've been able to use many of the valuable lessons that my parents have taught me. I am fortunate to have family members, coaches, and teammates around who can help me stay focused on the right things for me to be successful. For me, every day includes four things: God, family, academics, and football—in that order. And that's thanks to my family. Seeing how my parents have raised us and provided everything we can possibly need is a comforting feeling. I have been so blessed to have an amazing

support group, and knowing how passionate they are about God and us kids has inspired me."

Ironically, Tebow says that being a high-profile athlete actually has made serving easier. That's because opportunities to spend time with others and to share the gospel with them are always lurking around the corner. But Tebow still remains careful to convey a message of humility and selflessness to the various groups he addresses. He passionately points others to Jesus, who, according to Philippians 2:7, "emptied Himself by assuming the form of a slave, taking on the likeness of men."

"Jesus was the best leader ever, so you can learn everything about leadership from Him," Tebow says. "Seeing how He died on the cross for you and just learning from the best leader ever, you can just take that and apply it to your life in every aspect—not just leadership but also how you handle talking and interacting with people."

After his storied NCAA career, the Denver Broncos selected Tebow with the 25th overall pick in the first round of the 2010 NFL Draft. After seeing limited action as a rookie, he was given the chance to shine six games into the 2011 season. Tebow guided the Broncos to the playoffs and managed to excite fans with four come-from-behind victories. His playoff debut featured an 80-yard game-winning touchdown pass on the first play of overtime against the Pittsburgh Steelers.

Despite the heroics and a rabid fan base, Tebow was traded to the New York Jets after the Broncos signed Peyton Manning. A year later, he signed with the New England Patriots but was released before the start of the regular season. Although he continued to seek out employment in the NFL, Tebow simultaneously moved forward as an ESPN college football analyst.

No matter what Tebow does next, one thing is certain: Finding ways to reach out

and serve others will always be a part of his life. That includes working with his father's ministry—the Bob Tebow Evangelistic Association—and assisting more than forty national evangelists working in the Philippines. In 2010, he created the Tim Tebow Foundation and raised funds to build a children's hospital there.

"After football, I'd like to be involved again in the ministry in some way," Tebow says. "The Philippines are pretty special to me, and every year in high school up until college, I've been part of a group my dad would take there. It is a great experience. We go into medical clinics, hospitals, prisons, marketplaces, and schools. You preach and help out. We go to the orphanage and a lot of things like that. It's a great experience. I love going every year, and I can't wait until I go back.

"Then when you come back home, you're grateful for everything that God's given you, and you see how blessed you are."

Training Time

1. Tim Tebow's story is wrapped in many elements of humility, including the circumstances of his birth, his early life in the Philippines and his subsequent home-schooling background. What parts of your life story might help you to remain humble in the midst of personal success?

2. Tebow says, "Maybe I wasn't doing things that were bad in the eyes of the world, but I was still a sinner and I needed a Savior." Read Romans 3:23. When did you first realize the truth found in that passage? How did it change your life?

3. After winning the 2007 Heisman Trophy, Tebow could have easily given in to prideful thinking, but instead he chose to remain humble. Read Isaiah 2:11. How can you keep an attitude of humility regardless of the amount of success you achieve?

What are the dangers that often accompany pride?

4. Read Philippians 2:5–8. In what ways did Jesus display humility when He was on Earth? How might the average person have acted differently if he or she possessed the same divine heritage?

5. How does eradicating pride from your life make it easier to serve God and others? What are some ways that you might be able to rid your heart of pride?

6

Open Hearts

BETSY KING
Former LPGA Golfer

By this all people will know that you are My disciples, if you have love for one another.

John 13:35

It is not how much we do, but how much love we put in the doing. It is not how much we give, but how much love we put in the giving.

Mother Teresa

For nearly thirty years, Betsy King spent the majority of her time on the golf course. In most people's opinion—whether sports analysts or average fans—she did some pretty significant things in a career that resulted in thirty-four LPGA Tour event titles, six major champion-ships, and inductions into the World Golf Hall of Fame (1995) and the LPGA Hall of Fame (2000).

Yet while King was racking up every ac-
colade available within the realm of professional women's golf, a nagging doubt
lingered about the importance of her role
as an athlete and what life after sports
might look like. Those thoughts were
intensified after she read the book *Half
Time: Changing Your Game Plan from
Success to Significance* by Bob Buford.

"The book is about how you spend
the first half of your life building your
security and then you spend the second
half of your life doing something significant," King says. "When I was playing on
the tour, I always wondered what I was
going to do next. I didn't know what God
wanted me to do after the tour. I had a
hard time thinking about that."

Questions about a future away from
golf were the furthest things from King's
mind as a teenage girl growing up in the
midsized town of Redding, Pennsylvania,
about an hour's drive northwest of Philadelphia. The daughter of a physician,

she was eight years old when she started playing the game at a country club where her parents were members. As King entered high school, she also developed an interest in field hockey, softball, and basketball. She took her love of sports to Furman University in South Carolina, where she was a three-sport athlete. As a senior, she focused solely on golf, which propelled her to the professional ranks.

Previous to her time on the LPGA Tour, King was raised in a stereotypical religious home. She attended church every week and went to Sunday school. But King realized later in life that something was missing.

"We went to a mainline church where they didn't really talk about a personal relationship with Christ," King says. "Even though I learned some of the Bible stories, it was about more than knowing the stories, and I don't think I really understood. Yeah, I knew that Jesus died for the sin of the world, but I didn't personalize the fact that Jesus died for my sin."

King's spiritual paradigm slowly began to shift in December 1979 when Bill Lewis—founder of the FCA Golf Ministry—invited her to an FCA Pro-Am fund-raising event. Lewis was also from Redding and organized player-led Bible studies. He also had a book ministry that gave the golfers access to a wide array of Christian books and Bibles. A month later, King (who had been on the tour since 1977) attended a retreat for LPGA golfers called Tee Off, and it was there that she experienced God in a brand new way.

"I didn't make a profession of faith or commit my life to Christ until January 1980," King says. "Bruce Wilkinson was the speaker at the LPGA Fellowship retreat. There were maybe 30 of us there and he gave the chance to accept Christ after one of his talks."

Wilkinson, founder of the popular Walk Through the Bible Ministries, would go on to write the bestselling book *The Prayer of Jabez*. King would move on

to achieve greatness on the LPGA Tour. She won the US Open in 1989 and 1990 and claimed the LPGA Championship in 1992. King also won the Women's British Open in 1985, which at the time had yet to be declared a major.

King was also a stalwart of the United States Solheim Cup team, which competes biennially against the best golfers from Europe. She helped her team to victories in 1990, 1994, 1996, and 1998 and was part of the runner-up team in 1992. King was also honored to serve as the team captain in 2007 when the US team defeated the Europeans 16–12 in Halmstad, Sweden. Other awards that she stockpiled over her 28-year career include Rolex Player of the Year (1984, 1989, and 1993) as well as the Vare Trophy (1987 and 1993), which is given to the golfer with the lowest scoring average for the season.

After accepting Christ and subsequently getting more involved with the LPGA Fellowship, King made a natural

progression toward community outreach and ministry. Although she participated in service projects while part of a high school group called the Brotherhood Club, the concept of orchestrated serving was relatively new.

"Through the fellowship, we had some opportunities to serve," King says. "We did several Habitat for Humanity projects. We started by going to the mountains of Tennessee and working on houses there. Chris Stevens—who leads the Fellowship on the LPGA Tour—is from Knoxville, and this area was about an hour from Knoxville. We also spearheaded a project in Arizona one winter, in Guadalupe; and we raised the funds to build a house. We worked on the house for two weeks, and during that time, we probably had eighty players that came, between caddies and players and LPGA staff."

King also worked with Stevens and Drive for Life, which helped raise funds for a village in Tanzania. She traveled to

Romania in 1993 and 1994 to visit orphanages and assist an adoption agency seeking to place children with American families. King has also traveled to Korea and Japan, where she shared her testimony with various golf groups, and she has consistently participated in FCA golf camps as well.

In January 2005, King went to Honduras with LPGA golfer Hilary Lunke (and her husband, Tyler) to help build houses with World Vision, a humanitarian organization for which she has the utmost respect and admiration. Her association with the group has also helped her identify a greater understanding of serving.

"Serving is helping others without any expectations in return," King says. "I think about Mother Teresa. She helped people without any expectations. World Vision is a Christian organization, but it's not like every time they go to serve someone, there's an expectation that they have to share their faith. They work in some

countries where it's illegal to share your faith, but they are serving in the name of Christ because Christ called us to serve. If those opportunities arise, if someone asks, 'Why are you doing this?' then they can say, 'It's because of my love of Christ.'"

King also points to the example of Christ Himself, who first served the people's physical needs before speaking to their spiritual needs, with no prerequisites or demands to be met first.

"You can't go to someone who is starving to death and not help them physically and still expect them to want to listen to a message of Christ," claims King. "That's like saying, 'God loves you and I love you, but I'm not willing to help you.'"

As she continued to learn about serving, it became clear that her competitive golf career was nearing its end. In June 2005, her father was diagnosed with terminal cancer. Just three months later, he passed away. King was then faced with the challenge of caring for her mother, who

suffered with Alzheimer's disease, until she passed away in April 2007. In addition to handling these family crises, King was dealing with personal wear and tear, the natural result of nearly thirty years on the LPGA Tour. She retired in 2005, and shoulder surgery in 2006 effectively sealed the deal.

But that same year, King discovered new life within the golfing world when she was selected to be the 2007 US team captain at the prestigious Solheim Cup— the women's equivalent of the Ryder Cup. She was a natural fit for the head-to-head competition, having previously played in the event five times herself. And this time, it was going to be about much more than the game of golf.

"I decided I wanted to use that platform to do something," King reveals. "I read a book called *The End of Poverty: Economic Possibilities of Our Time* by Jeffrey Sachs. So I called Dana Buck, my contact at World Vision, and told him I wanted to do something, and I felt like I

was being led to do something in Africa. He told me I needed to go over there, and they were putting together a group of women to go over there. So I ended up going there in 2006."

After an exploratory trip that took King to Tanzania, Kenya, Rwanda, and Zambia, she returned with the inspiration for a nonprofit organization appropriately named Golf Fore Africa. The organization's purpose is "to raise funds and awareness within the golf community to help those who have been infected or are affected by AIDS." The LPGA lent its support to King's first project in Rwanda, and to date close to $200,000 in donations have been collected.

"So basically, we exist to be a fundraising body to help people who are already on the ground doing the work," King says. "We'll go over there to make sure that what we've raised is being used effectively. But the most effective thing to do is to give your money to help those that

are there that have the expertise. That's a part of service."

"I'm being an advocate," she continues. "I can speak out. I've gone and seen it firsthand, and I think that's why they want us to go. That's what God calls us to do. It's like when Jesus healed the paralytic who wanted to stick around with Him, He said, 'No, go home, and tell your family what God's done for you and how He's had mercy on you.' That's what I feel I'm called to do too—to talk about what I've seen and to be an advocate for those people."

For King, it's become quite personal. Because of her experiences in Africa, it's more to her than just helping strangers in a strange land. King has met with men, women, and children impacted by disease, poverty, and war. Those one-on-one human connections have fueled her passion to serve the ones that Jesus referred to in Matthew 25:40 as "the least of these."

"We helped one woman who was twenty-four years old and was blind," King shares. "She was the head of her household, and she had five siblings. World Vision was providing seeds so that she could plant Irish potatoes in her little plot of land. So we basically did that. We had all of the villagers watching us and laughing at us and then some of the women jumped in and helped us with the hoeing, and they had the babies strapped on their backs. But in that situation, it's more about good will. There's a language barrier, and yet you're showing them that you care. I think that brings dignity to people. What we heard when we met with people was that we came all that way to see them and that showed we cared about them."

King has learned that serving can show the love of Jesus to others without the use of one single word. She has also discovered that taking others along for the ride can have a similar impact and open the door for evangelism. Not all of the

people King has brought to Africa have been believers, and some who believe have a level of faith that is evident but not fully developed. In both instances, King has been amazed at how the powerful nature of serving others opens the hearts of those tag-along servants.

"When you have people like professional golfers who make these trips, they're getting a lot of their needs met," King says. "You're bringing them into a cause that's bigger than them. That often gives you an opportunity to share your faith. It changes their heart. It's a common ground where you can come together. The people that went with us to Africa, most of them weren't believers. So you're putting them in a situation where they get to see Christians who are different, and they're helping people, and that just might be the introduction that takes them a step along the way."

Not only does King hope to put a dent in many of Africa's problems, but she

would also love to see the next generation of servants rise up and get involved with similar worthy and life-changing causes. "When you see what other people are going through," she says, "it tends to put your life in perspective."

For instance, in Rwanda, King saw the tragic results of poverty and AIDS set against a hideous backdrop of war and genocide. She met one Rwandan employed by World Vision who had lost seventy members of her family to the genocide. Amazingly, this woman had courageously moved forward to accept a position titled Head of Healing, Peace, and Reconciliation.

"People who come to Rwanda think they have a lot of problems," King says. "But when they see what the people there have to forgive, it makes their problems seem small. I mean they have to forgive the people that have killed their families and their friends that are now coming back into society, and they're living next

to them. That's what they're facing now. There are so many things that you learn through serving."

King has also seen the positive impact that the United States government has facilitated through a $30 billion pledge made by President George W. Bush in 2003. She was pleased to hear the president commit an additional $30 billion for AIDS during the 2008 State of the Union address. Because of King's captaincy with the winning Solheim Cup team, she actually had the chance to thank President Bush in person.

As pleased as she was to see that kind of compassion coming from the White House, King has been even more gratified by her opportunity to work alongside and generate support for the unsung heroes of this battle against social injustice.

"I am so inspired by the faith of the Christians who are there every day in the midst of poverty, trying to make a difference," King says. "I think you're

just inspired by those you're serving or those you're serving with—inspired by the beauty of the people. You definitely get a lot more back than what you give. As believers, we're all called to serve. We're all called to witness, to share our story. We're also called to be a part of the community of believers. But He also calls us to a life of service. So really, if you want to be obedient, you need to be serving."

Training Time

1. Betsy King talks about the need for security versus the struggle for significance. How important is security (financial, relational, spiritual) to you? How often do you find yourself thinking about being a person of significance?

2. Why should you expect nothing in return when serving others? What are some ways that Jesus demonstrated

this philosophy throughout His ministry of healing and teaching?

3. Read Matthew 25:31–46. What imagery comes to mind when you hear the phrase "the least of these"? What does the disparity between Jesus's two responses tell you about God's emphasis on serving those in need?

4. Read John 13:35. How do Jesus's words in this passage contrast with what many nonbelievers think of today's church body? Why is it important for us to show love to one another as well as to those outside of the church walls?

5. What are some ways that serving can change the heart of the servant? How can serving open the hearts of those being served? Can you describe a time when you've seen one or both of these scenarios played out in your own acts of service?

journal

Thanks

Fellowship of Christian Athletes would like to give honor and glory to our Lord and Savior Jesus Christ for the opportunities we have been given to impact so many lives and for everyone who has come alongside us in this ministry.

The four core values are at the heart of what we do and teach. Many people have helped make this series of books on these values a reality. We extend a huge thanks to Chad Bonham for his many hours of hard work in interviewing, writing, compiling, and editing. These books would

not have been possible without him. Thanks also to Chad's wife, Amy, and his three sons, Lance, Cole, and Quinn.

We also want to thank the following people and groups for their vital contributions: Tony Dungy, Jackie Cook, the Indianapolis Colts, Pat Williams, Andrew Herdliska, the Orlando Magic, Tim Tebow, Zack Higbee, John Hines, University of Florida Media Relations, Betsy King, Elana Meyers-Taylor, Kyle Korver, Garin Narain, the Atlanta Hawks, Klayton Korver, and Dave Pond.

Thanks to the entire FCA staff, who every day faithfully serve coaches and athletes. Thanks to our CEO and president, Les Steckel, for believing in this project. Thanks to the National Support Center staff: Jeff Martin, Shea Vailes, and Dan Britton. Thanks also to everyone at Revell Books.

Impacting the World for Christ Through Sports

Since 1954, the Fellowship of Christian Athletes has challenged athletes and coaches to impact the world for Jesus Christ. FCA is cultivating Christian principles in local communities nationwide by encouraging, equipping, and empowering others to serve as examples and make a difference. FCA reaches more than two million people annually on the professional, college, high school, junior high,

and youth levels. Through FCA's Four Cs of Ministry—Coaches, Campus, Camp, and Community—and the shared passion for athletics and faith, lives are changed for current and future generations.

Fellowship of Christian Athletes
8701 Leeds Road • Kansas City, MO 64129
www. fca.org • fca@fca.org • 1-800-289-0909

Fellowship of Christian Athletes
Competitor's Creed

I am a Christian first and last.

I am created in the likeness of God Almighty to bring Him glory.

I am a member of Team Jesus Christ.

I wear the colors of the cross.

I am a Competitor now and forever.

I am made to strive, to strain, to stretch and to succeed in the arena of competition.

I am a Christian Competitor and as such, I face my challenger with the face of Christ.

I do not trust in myself.

I do not boast in my abilities or believe in my own strength.

I rely solely on the power of God.

I compete for the pleasure of my Heavenly Father, the honor of Christ and the reputation of the Holy Spirit.

My attitude on and off the field is above reproach—my conduct beyond criticism.

Whether I am preparing, practicing or playing, I submit to God's authority and those He has put over me.

I respect my coaches, officials, team-mates, and competitors out of respect for the Lord.

My body is the temple of Jesus Christ.

I protect it from within and without.

Nothing enters my body that does not honor the Living God.

My sweat is an offering to my Master. My soreness is a sacrifice to my Savior.

I give my all—all the time.

I do not give up. I do not give in. I do not give out.

I am the Lord's warrior—a competitor by conviction and a disciple of determination.

I am confident beyond reason because my confidence lies in Christ.

The results of my effort must result in His glory.

Let the competition begin.

Let the glory be God's.

© Fellowship of Christian
Athletes, 2015

Sign the Creed • Go to www.fca.org

Fellowship
of Christian Athletes
Coach's Mandate

Pray as though nothing of eternal value
is going to happen in my athletes' lives
unless God does it.

Prepare each practice and game as giving
"my utmost for His highest."

Seek not to be served by my athletes for
personal gain, but seek to serve them as
Christ served the church.

Be satisfied not with producing a good record, but with producing good athletes.

Attend carefully to my private and public walk with God, knowing that the athlete will never rise to a standard higher than that being lived by the coach.

Exalt Christ in my coaching, trusting the Lord will then draw athletes to Himself.

Desire to have a growing hunger for God's Word, for personal obedience, for fruit of the spirit and for saltiness in competition.

Depend solely upon God for transformation—one athlete at a time.

Preach Christ's word in a Christ-like demeanor, on and off the field of competition.

Recognize that it is impossible to bring glory to both myself and Christ at the same time.

Allow my coaching to exude the fruit of the Spirit, thus producing Christ-like athletes.

Trust God to produce in my athletes His chosen purposes, regardless of whether the wins are readily visible.

Coach with humble gratitude, as one privileged to be God's coach.

© Fellowship of Christian Athletes, 2015. Revised from "The Preacher's Mandate."

Impacting The World
For Christ Through Sports

Since 1954, the Fellowship of Christian Athletes has challenged athletes and coaches to impact the world for Jesus Christ. FCA is cultivating Christian principles in local communities nationwide by encouraging, equipping, and empowering others to serve as examples and make a difference. FCA reaches more than 2 million people annually on the professional, college, high school, junior high, and youth levels. Through FCA's Four Cs of Ministry—coaches, campus, camps, and community— and the shared passion for athletics and faith, lives are changed for current and future generations.

Fellowship of Christian Athletes
8701 Leeds Road • Kansas City, MO 64129
www.fca.org • fca@fca.org • 1-800-289-0909